Choose to Enjoy

Jennifer Simpson

Published by New Generation Publishing in 2023

Copyright © Jennifer Simpson 2023

First Edition

The author asserts the moral right under the Copyright, Designs and Patents Act 1988 to be identified as the author of this work.

All Rights reserved. No part of this publication may be reproduced, stored in a retrieval system or transmitted, in any form or by any means without the prior consent of the author, nor be otherwise circulated in any form of binding or cover other than that which it is published and without a similar condition being imposed on the subsequent purchaser.

ISBN
Paperback   978-1-80369-902-8
ebook   978-1-80369-903-5

www.newgeneration-publishing.com

New Generation Publishing

Contents

Note from Jennifer	iv
Introduction	1
1 Rainbows	6
2 No 8	10
3 Newcastle	14
4 Facebook	17
5 Morning Preparation	19
6 Dream 1	22
7 Dream 2	28
8 Lights in the Long Dark Tunnel	31
9 The Blessing of A B C	37
10 Perfect Timing	42
11 An Unexpected Privilege	46
12 Give, Take Away, but Give Back Even More!	50
Conclusion	54
Thank You	57
Contact	58

Choose to Enjoy

Note from Jennifer

This little book has been written solely in response to God's prompting on Christmas Day 2021.

The Lord specifically said, '*Write to bring glory to me.*' So, as a response to this and a desire to do as the Shorter Catechism says, 'Glorify God and enjoy Him forever.'

I began to record my story.

At this time, my husband and I were entering the final stage of a four-and-a-half-year life-changing situation; mentally exhausted but spiritually overflowing.

I realised that Satan's plan was to cause us much harm, but rather, God had allowed it for our good. **'As for you, you meant evil against me, but God meant it for good'** (Joseph to his brothers in Genesis 50:20).

Most of the book was written in a few weeks, then left unfinished for a time, dipping in and out to write a little more. Each time a battle soared against the forces of evil! I kept hearing, 'What a stupid idea to write a book,' clearly each time – an attack of the enemy to give up and make sure glory was not given to God. I battled on, praying for strength and protection to keep going in a bid to glorify Jesus. Sixteen months later I finally finished!

I pray God *will* be glorified and your heart blessed as you read of the grace and goodness of our Sovereign Father.

Introduction

September 2014

It was an exciting time in our lives; numerous cards of 'good wishes' fell onto our front door mat.

Enthusiastically we tore open yet another envelope to find out who the next individual or couple were to wish us God's blessing on the new ministry He had called us to. This card was different! I pondered over the words: 'I will choose to enjoy the journey that God has set before me.' Of course, I'll enjoy this journey; why wouldn't I? Surely this new vocation couldn't be that hard. Or would it?

Of all the greetings cards, this one would not leave my memory. In fact, the words became so embedded in my heart that I had no other option except to frame it. So, for the last almost nine years it has remained in a prominent position in our home. Never did I realise the importance of this quotation at this time; but God knew! **'For I know the plans I have for you, declares the Lord…'** (Jeremiah 29:11)

September 2016

Excitement was mounting for the church ladies' weekend event. Many had booked in; it would be a blessed time of teaching, fellowship and strengthening of relationships.

The organising team of three decided to leave a small gift for each lady on their hotel pillow. It ended up as three little gifts, one being a little insignificant candle, to become very significant in the following, unknown, painful years of our lives.

A candle looks radiant in a dark corner. Yes, that's it, the theme of the ladies' weekend was confirmed! 'Radiant.' God highlighted to me in Psalm 34:5, **'Those who look to him are radiant and their faces shall never be ashamed.'** My personal desire to be radiant for Jesus was realised and became my prayer for myself and the ladies who would attend the weekend.

The 'radiant'-themed weekend in the Roe Valley came and went and was truly blessed by God in every way. Each detail, according to His will and not least, the humble little candle gift! Attached to them with raffia – a simple handwritten Bible verse which had been randomly placed on each lady's bed.

My randomly placed candle displayed the beautiful verse from Psalm 56:3, **'When I am afraid, I put my trust in you.'** Not designated to me by chance but by the amazing sovereign hand of our King!

Over the following months I sought to ask God to make me a radiant disciple for His glory.

Spring 2017

My Bible devotions were focused on Paul's letter to the church in Philippi – that tiny, yet highly powerful book of Philippians. Verse ten in chapter three caught my eye. I recited it over and over, knowing deep in my heart this was what God was asking me to do; to know Him better! My thinking was instantly transported to the ladies' weekend theme – 'radiant' – I realised my Heavenly Father was revealing to me that I could never be radiant without knowing Jesus in a deeper and more intimate way.

'That I may know him and the power of his resurrection and may share his sufferings, becoming like him in his death' (Philippians 3:10). A simple, straightforward verse to understand, but not so straightforward and simple to live. I found myself in a struggle – I wanted to know Jesus better, but I was not sure if I was up for the suffering bit!

* * * * *

I prayed a prayer. A prayer to ask our Heavenly Father that Matthew and I would be the godly son and daughter that He required and that we would come to know Him more.

* * * * *

Over the next weeks I sought my journey into knowing

God in a deeper way, albeit lodging distinctively in my mind the possibility of suffering ahead – something I had known little about.

Little did I know…

June 2017

The suffering began...

The trauma began…

The unknown began…

The waiting began…

It was a beautiful, spring morning, but just in an instant our world was thrown into turmoil and disarray.

Our immediate reaction was, 'What is going on? What is this about? I don't understand.' My darling husband and I sat down on our settee and holding hands I heard, 'I'm sorry about this, it is for your own good, I am in control.' Dear reader, you have guessed correctly! It certainly was the still small voice of our precious Saviour. In an instant our home filled with the presence of Jesus and a peace that we could never explain. **'And the peace of God, which surpasses all understanding, will guard your hearts and your minds in Christ Jesus'** (Philippians 4:7).

Praise God, our hearts and minds were being guarded for whatever lay ahead. However precious and beautiful as this encounter was, it did not minimalise the trauma and reality of what was happening all around us. We really were in a whirl; but in it with

Jesus and with His knowledge and consent.

The days that were to follow were packed with numbness, sleepless nights, tears, questions, prayer, seeking God and His word and circling in a whirlwind of an all-consuming horrific reality. We had no answers to our questions – What? How? Why? When?

The following chapters recall the blessings, protection, care, counsel, and guiding hand of our Almighty Father over an unknown and painful four and a half years of waiting.

1
Rainbows

June 2017

Matthew and I love to be by the sea and experience the peace, calm and de-stressing power that it brings. So, with Oscar, our little Lasa Apso and that special candle verse attached to the kitchen roll holder, off we set (with Jesus) in our motorhome and headed for the peaceful coast.

Fresh air is always a good thing and recently had become one of our best friends!

We were barely five minutes out walking along the coastal path when out of nowhere the rain clouds gathered and suddenly, we were walking under a deluge of water from the heavens. We ran as fast as our weak and burdened legs could take us, back towards the motorhome. Just a few metres from our vehicle, as quickly as it started, the rain ended. 'Thank you, Lord, you knew we needed a longer walk.' So, in a totally different direction we continued our refreshing but rather damp walk, this time up the hill towards Whitehead village from the car park.

Heavily panting and only halfway up the steep path, a

voice said, 'Jennifer, turn around.' It was that still small voice again! Holding onto Matthew to keep me steady, we turned around; the most spectacular rainbow we had ever seen was right in front of our faces, perfect in its seven-colour and arc formation. It looked soft and inviting. I reached out; I thought I could grasp it.

We stood embracing for several minutes as we took in the splendour of the sight; yet again, that still small voice reminding us of His presence. This would be an ongoing sign that He would be with us and be faithful to us in the tough days, months, and unforeseen years (to us) that lay ahead. What an amazing Heavenly Father! These first few days had certainly been no easy pathway, but God in His love, compassion and mercy was helping us to try **'to enjoy the journey set before us'.**

When the rainbow faded, we proceeded on up the hill. Instantly, we realised had we been twenty seconds later, we would never have seen the rainbow. A row of upcoming houses would have completely blocked our view. Our Sovereign Father was indeed looking after us. This was the first of numerous accounts of His care, direction, and presence during the years to follow.

During this same walk, our son rang and after a conversation with his dad, he chatted to me. All I remember him saying was, 'Mum, God is in control.' It most certainly did not appear to be the case, but deep down we knew it was! He *would* take us through a very long, dark and scary tunnel, as it later transpired.

Rainbows had become a sign from our Heavenly Father on dozens of occasions over the next years – even when it looked like there was not a drop of rain for miles around, in God's timing that rainbow appeared. They were a strong reminder of God's faithful, protecting, controlling, and guiding hand upon our situation.

Please allow me to share one more 'rainbow' experience!

We were coming from Belfast towards Lisburn; we were both afraid and anxious, doubting God's help and feeling very much another satanic attack upon our lives. After all, we had been totally and completely thrown into the hands of our Sovereign Father; we were stripped of everything, and the enemy knew it.

Exhausted, lost and at the feet of Jesus, Matthew prayed for the Lord to show us that He was still with us. Ten minutes later in the car park we were pleading with God to answer our prayer, or we could not go on.

Walking around Hillsborough Lake that day, holding hands and resting in the calming gentle hands of Jesus we walked into a rain shower (yet again!) that poured out of nowhere, sheltering under the trees and then running back to the car as fast as our middle age allowed. The rain stopped; just like that! To catch our breath, we saw a bench nearby and gladly flopped down on it to rest.

But wait a minute! We looked at each other – the seat was dry. It had just poured out of the heavens; how come the bench was dry? Did God know we needed the rest? Well, maybe. The real reason was in the sky.

Yes, you're right – a rainbow. If the seat had been wet, we would have darted on past – God wanted to bless us! God had answered Matthew's prayer request; He *was* still with us. He performed a miracle right there at Hillsborough Lake to show us. What slow learners we are. What incredible patience God has.

And so, the rainbow sightings continued, year on year while we waited. Each one for a special reason and each in perfect timing. What a Faithful God!

2
No 8

Summer 2017

It is in an ideal location, looks like a quiet little community, it is handy to the town and, to top it all, just a two-minute walk to the 11-mile-long Lagan towpath. Lots of running, walking, cycling, chilling, chatting and birdwatching could potentially be enjoyed.

The house was small but adequate, sporting a decent back garden and detached garage and shed. Although very dated and not housing any of today's modern facilities, it would be an excellent purchase for a first-time buyer. The bidding started and before long our daughter had secured her first ever home. We were delighted for her and knew that with much TLC, organising and persistence she would achieve her dreams for this property.

In the autumn the keys were handed over and No 8 became her first large practical project.

'Dad and Mum, feel free to have a few days in the house for a break,' our daughter insisted. 'Really? At your new house? But…'

Yes, there were many buts!

Despite the buts, we took our daughter up on the offer, packed our bags and headed to Lisburn to have a break in this 'state-of-the-art' property.

As I said, there were many buts.

The house needed a good clean; I mean, a top-to-bottom clean. There were no blinds or curtains. There was no heating or hot water (but there was a very dated 1980's open fire, which could provide both!). In the bathroom was a shower, although it didn't work. Thankfully, in the kitchen was a free-standing working cooker – oh no, our daughter had just sold this! So, we had no cooker, either.

I know what you're thinking, and you are correct – no microwave, dishwasher, fridge, bed, dining table, TV.

We had a lot to sort, clean and scrub before we were going to get this break. Sleeves rolled up, attired in our old clothes, worship music playing, we set to work and by night-time we had our clean and humble home for the week sorted.

It's unbelievable what people leave behind them when they sell a house. The attic, garage and shed were full of many treasures. We retrieved a floor lamp, mats for the floor, an electric clock, an antique (1950's) one-burner electric hob (still working), a huge electric retro kettle, two retro comfy fireside chairs, crockery, cutlery and saucepans… we had all we needed. God was very good.

A quick drive to the local Tesco and petrol station

provided the fuel and food we would use for the few days. We settled in, aware of the warmth and presence of our loving Jesus by our side.

We had come prepared with a bag of books, our Bibles, journals, and podcasts at the ready.

With the heat of a blazing fire in that old, dated fireplace and the comfort of a big mug of tea and no doubt something sweet, we sat and relaxed in the beautiful presence of our Sovereign Father.

Over refreshments and before retiring to our air bed upstairs, we chatted about our surroundings. The words that engulfed us both were from the words in Hebrews 13:5, **'Keep your life free from love of money and be content with what you have, for he has said, "I will never leave you nor forsake you."'**

We were truly content – content in Jesus and over the week we often thought of this verse, continuing to recognise our total contentment and happiness with our temporary arrangement for the week. More incredibly, content as we journeyed through a traumatic situation that God had permitted us to endure.

By the end of our time at No 8 we both knew that if this was to be the way God wanted us to live in a permanent capacity, it would indeed be perfect and beautiful, being His will for us. These days taught us much about our contentment in Christ; it is not about who we are, or what our situation is, but rather, how we understand who Jesus really is.

It must be said of many missionaries and Christian workers from times past that they had a complete contentment in Christ to live in the many diverse, and in our western terms, 'unhabitable' homes.

It is likely that most of us have heard testimonies of these faithful servants living in mud houses, houses with leaking tin roofs, holes in the windows and doors letting in vermin of all types, crawling around their feet, in the bed, cupboards and even amongst the kitchen crockery and bathroom sink. Yuk! Yet this was daily life for years, for many.

There were few modern comforts – certainly no microwave, dishwasher, washing machine and perhaps even no bathroom.

Paul, from a lonely and unpleasant prison cell said, **'Not that I am speaking of being in need, for I have learned in whatever situation I am to be content'** (Philippians 4:11).

What a challenge Paul's words and life are to us as we live in the 21st century of 'must haves' and 'can't do withouts'.

It certainly is not things, fame, position, or any worldly asset that make us content. It is, however, our total trust in our Sovereign King who rules over all. Praise Him that we can be complete in Him, lacking nothing.

'The Lord is my shepherd; I shall not want' (Psalm 23:1).

3
Newcastle

July 2017

Our other daughter lived in the Co Down and had blessed us with our third grandson in May; needless to say, we wanted to be with her as much as possible to be with this new little miracle.

We packed the motorhome and off we set, intending to stay for a few days to help where needed. What a joy, during huge trauma to be able to smile and find much comfort in the joy of this new and precious wee guy. God is very good, and His timing is always perfect.

On a warm pleasant day, Matthew and I, along with Oscar, headed to the coast. It was a relatively short trip – thirty minutes or so from the Co Down village.

A walk on the beach is always top priority when we get to the coast. Especially with Oscar. He hated the ocean but loved running along the sand, clutching the ball or driftwood in his mouth as we would walk.

We strolled along the seaweed-cluttered beach until

the Murlough Bay beach, pedestrian entrance. Our conversation totally focused and saturated on our situation. We cried, we prayed, we smiled as Oscar frolicked around in the sand, and we gave thanks for the safe arrival of our grandson, but our hearts were very heavy.

On our return walk back towards Newcastle we were strengthened as we reminded ourselves of God's Word and His consistent promise to us that He was in control – 'I know the plan' – it kept us sane! Our son rang and we engaged in a loving, God-centred conversation with him and his lovely wife.

We, being human had our list of 'prayer requests' but as we came off the phone that day, the Lord spoke again, in that same still voice. Before I knew what was happening, Matthew started to pray. He prayed a prayer that I could not pray; a prayer I was sure I could never pray; that we would accept God's will. I'm ashamed to say, it was many months in the future until I, too, could pray this prayer.

'Your will be done,' – it did not come easy and certainly not without tears, but in total surrender to my Sovereign King, I meant it.

The peace, joy, comfort, liberation, grace – the sheer happiness that followed, was something I had not witnessed before. For me, in my stubborn and rebellious nature – a huge 'handing over'.

The 'handing over' was not a one off, 'now it's done' act. This was simply the start (in this unique suffering), being repeated countless times since. As a sinner, saved by God's grace, it will also need to be repeated frequently for the rest of my life.

Matthew had continued to pray that day on the beach, that not only would we accept His will, but that God's name would be glorified in this dismal situation. I remember thinking that was impossible! I just wanted my prayer request answered. That this thing would be over by the end of the summer, and we could get our lives back. This, disappointingly for me, was not God's will for us.

This concept about God's name being glorified played on my mind for days, weeks. I was further plagued by the words in the shorter catechism which asks and answers, 'What is man's chief end? To glorify God and enjoy Him forever.' Finally, my prayer: 'Lord, glorify your name through this test you have allowed to envelop our lives. I do not know how, but since you are in control, I trust you to work it out.'

This was the start of a beautiful awakening as to how God could and would be glorified through our lives, albeit throughout and because of a harsh time of suffering.

4
Facebook

Little by little the Lord showed me ways in which I could glorify Him while we waited for Him to reveal His purpose in our lives. Hopefully, also learning more about continuing to glorify Jesus, even when our 'now disrupted' lives would return to normal.

I was sitting one day wasting time on Facebook (as you do), scrolling, and looking to see what was happening in the world around me and in the lives of friends. May I add, Facebook friends also; many of whom I no longer would see or even know where they lived or worked or anything about them.

God started to speak to me!

'Why do you waste so much time on Facebook?'

I answered simply by saying, 'I don't really spend that much time on Facebook; not compared to others!'

That day, God showed me that what others did was not what He may want me to do. Also, when I sat and approximately calculated how many little five-minute slots per day I *did* go onto Facebook, I was stunned!

The horrible, sad discovery was that I spent longer

engaging on Facebook than I did in engaging with God's word. I was highly convicted and made this the focus of my prayer requests.

The realisation of Facebook dependence became very clear; I did need this prayer to be answered. Sooner, rather than later. Like any obsession, it takes time to let go. With the help of the Holy Spirit, Facebook through time, became a tool to glorify God rather than a distraction from God. Being free from the hold of Facebook was truly liberating. Now, I had more time to focus on the things in life that needed my attention.

When God started to challenge me about using Facebook as a tool to glorify Him – it sounded perfect for me. Now I would focus on my new determination to filter out futile usage. This would be a fabulous opportunity to glorify Jesus, so long as He would give me the direction.

That He did! Now, I predominately use Facebook to remind viewers of the personal truths for us in God's word. It may be a simple and insignificant means to bring Him glory, but it is His command, so I know that He will bless it for the glory of His name!

5
Morning Preparation

One day, I found myself overwhelmed and in a very dark and difficult place; the presence of evil hovered around me and the peace and presence of Jesus seemed far away.

I immediately called out and kept repeating the name of Jesus. I pleaded for God to come and cover me and our home in His blood and to help me somehow to lift the seemingly very heavy shield of faith. Eventually, evil departed, and the beautiful peace of Jesus filled my heart. This was an experience I will never forget!

At this time God was reminding me of the importance of having His armour placed tightly around my life and that constantly being covered by His blood is paramount. (Dream one, recorded in the next chapter reinforced this truth in my mind.)

Daily I started to clutch each piece of the armour and literally place it physically onto my body, pleading Jesus' name as I did so. Satan *hated* it and eventually ran away and left me alone, until the next time, which would be just around the corner.

Since this time, when I feel the presence of evil,

temptation, fear and anger, or any other dart from the enemy, I find myself going back to this important truth highlighted to me. I plead for the covering of Jesus' blood and ask God to enable me to firmly strap His armour around my life. Also, to give the needed strength to hold up the very large and heavy shield of faith. There were many occasions when it felt like that – too hard to keep the faith.

I recall how I had often functioned through life without the daily protection of the armour – doing service in my own strength and letting pride have its horrible way.

What a treasure to have learned to take hold of this essential armour, putting each piece in place and equipping me for whatever the day would toss my way.

As God's children it is an incredible gift to help us fight the forces of the evil one. Evil forces come in various forms, causing us to doubt, be fearful or anxious, to give up and despair – making us feel vulnerable, rejected, cheated and alone. What a liar he is! John 8:44 says, **'He was a murderer from the beginning and does not stand in the truth, because there is no truth in him. When he lies, he speaks out of his own character, for he is a liar and the father of lies.'**

To adorn the armour of God is not a one off, but a daily activity. Sometimes an hourly activity!

I am slowly learning to create a habit each morning before my feet hit the floor – To ask God to help me put that beautiful armour on and plead the covering of His blood on my life and the lives of my family.

What an amazing provision! Giving strength, courage, protection, wisdom, and masses more, to take me through victoriously, both in the mundane and the more meaningful daily tasks of life.

'Finally, be strong in the Lord and in the strength of his might. Put on the whole armour of God, that you may be able to stand against the schemes of the devil. For we do not wrestle against flesh and blood, but against the rulers, against the authorities, against the cosmic powers over this present darkness, against the spiritual forces of evil in the heavenly places. Therefore, take up the whole armour of God, that you may be able to withstand in the evil day and having done all, to stand firm. Stand therefore, having fastened on the belt of truth and having put on the breastplate of righteousness and as shoes for your feet, having put on the readiness given by the gospel of peace. In all circumstances take up the shield of faith, with which you can extinguish all the flaming darts of the evil one and take the helmet of salvation and the sword of the Spirit, which is the word of God, praying at all times in the Spirit, with all prayer and supplication.' Ephesians 6 10-18

6
Dream 1

February 2019

I woke early in the morning; an absolutely memorable, detailed and significant dream was imbedded deep in my memory. I shuddered as I recalled, yet smiled and worshipped, the power of Jesus was right here in our home with us both.

In the dream I was in an empty room; an upstairs room, accessed by a wooden stairway. I was standing chatting to my sisters, relaxed and happy – everything was normal.

Through time, someone came up the stairs. Their footsteps on the bare wooden floor were unmistaken, turning the round knob on the door they entered and disrupted our calm, sisterly conversation.

This very pleasant and seemingly happy person started to chat to us – just general chit chat. I, being one of the more talkative of us sisters proceeded to engage in a two-way conversation with this stranger.

As time went on, the chatting turned to many questions asked by this individual, questions on the Bible, God and the gospel. I tried to answer as best as my theological understanding allowed me. And of course, not least by the help and instant wisdom from the Holy Spirit.

However, I could hear a resistance in their voice, a mocking, a disbelief, a questioning, perhaps a godless mind behind it all. This noticeably became stronger and more specific, and the individual started to speak in a louder, more pronounced, and seemingly authoritative tone. I was afraid, I didn't like what I was witnessing. At this stage I was now alone with this, now openly arrogant, God-hating, evil person – I cried out to God for help.

Every answer I gave at this stage was truly not of self, I couldn't possibly have so rapidly articulated the answers. God was sheltering me in His wings and as each dart was thrown, He gave me the remembrance and authority of His precious word. I recited every scripture verse I could in relation to each question and now, as it had transpired, I was standing in enemy territory.

Exhausted, yet with a spirit of calm and resilience I watched as the attacker opened a door in the room; a door that I thought was just a cupboard. I was wrong, very wrong. Inside were a group of young people all chatting and appeared to be pleasant and friendly (just as the enemy had done when they first entered the room). They looked out and smiled at me but as rapidly as they appeared, they too started to ask questions and before long the group began to mock and laugh – their excessive anger was a clear indication that they were haters of anything to do with the Kingdom of God.

Between them all, the noise was overpowering, I could no longer think clearly, my legs were starting to leave me and with every effort I could muster I continued to repeat God's word – it kept me going, until I heard that still small voice, once again. 'Jennifer, just worship me,' was the gentle and compassionate command. I did!

I sang in my untrained, wavering, yet strongest singing voice the first hymn that my precious Jesus brought into my mind:

> 'What can wash away my sin, nothing but the
> blood of Jesus,
> What can make me whole again, nothing but
> the blood of Jesus,
> Oh, precious is the flow, that makes me white
> as snow, no other fount I know, nothing but
> the blood of Jesus.'

I proceeded to sing through each verse – some people left. There was a battle going on!

Then I sang:

> 'Would you be free from your burden of sin,
> There's power in the blood, power in the
> blood,
> Come for a cleansing to Calvary's tide,
> There's wonderful power in the blood.'

Although my eyes were closed, I was aware that the

noisy din around me had died down. I kept bellowing as loud as my lungs allowed.

> *'There is power, power, wonder working power, in the blood of the lamb, there is power, power wonder working power in the precious blood of the lamb.'*

I was now in full flow and had total liberty in praising God and lifting Him up, protecting myself by His blood from the evil around me. Albeit, somewhat diminishing in its forceful presence in the room. I was aware more people had left – smiles wiped off their faces and sneering lips closed.

I could feel the presence of Almighty God!

I proceeded to sing:

> 'In the name of Jesus, in the name of Jesus,
> we have the Victory.
> In the name of Jesus, in the name of Jesus
> demons will have to flee.
> Who can tell what God can do? Who can tell
> of His love for me? In the name of Jesus,
> Jesus, we have the Victory.'

A lot more people left. By this stage I was so thrilled at the amazing power of God that my joy flowed over. I had almost forgot about the people.

Still, I was aware of a few livid God haters remaining in the room, so the praise continued:

'Oh Lord my God, when I in awesome wonder,
Consider all the works Thy hands have made,
I see the stars I hear the rolling thunder,
Thy power throughout the universe displayed.

Then sings my soul (I was now in heaven!) my saviour God to thee,
How great thou art, how great thou art,
Then sings my soul my saviour God to Thee,
How great thou art, how great thou art.'

Before I started the next verse, I opened my eyes – many in the side room had left; the initial jeerer – anger leapt from his eyes!

Second verse…

Last verse – peace and calm filled the room; I continued with my now hoarse, yet determined and joyful voice.

'When Christ shall come, with shout of acclamation,
And take me home, what joy shall fill my heart,
Then I shall bow, in humble adoration,
And then proclaim, my God, how great Thou art.'

I peeped for a few seconds into the room; the side room was nearly empty, and the original first visitor was heading for the door.

> 'Then sings my soul, my saviour God to Thee,
> How great Thou art how great Thou art,
> Then sings my soul my saviour God to Thee,
> *How great Thou art, how great Thou art.'*

Even more exhausted, yet 'soaring with the eagles', I stopped singing. looked around and listened. Not a human person in sight! Not a human sound to be heard! God's presence was tangible – His still small voice whispered 'peace'.

The dream ended.

I had overcome! By the power of His word and praise to our only victorious King.

The enemy *hates* praise and worship to the Sovereign God of the universe. Be encouraged, dear friend. Keep praising through singing and prayerful praise. It will lift your focus to our great God and will bring His beautiful, abiding and unexplained peace. It will combat the forces of the enemy.

'When I am afraid, I put my trust in you. In God, whose word I praise. In God I trust, I will not be afraid. What can flesh do to me?' (Psalm 56:3-4.)

7
Dream 2

July 2019

I was on a long and narrow boat (it looked like the inside of a plane) with my daughter, other family, friends, and strangers. We were on a journey to somewhere exotic! For us to reach this beautiful yet unknown destination we had firstly to sail for 25 minutes up a very long and narrow waterway before entering the open ocean.

As we sailed up this section of narrow water the captain spoke through the speaker. He said, 'Just before we come out into the ocean we will go through a swell on the tide. This may be somewhat scary for you, but it is routine and a necessity for you to get to your destination. When the water swells and comes into the boat, you can stand on your seats if you wish, but be calm, all will be perfectly fine.'

Minutes later it happened! The water came gushing into the boat and we were soon under water. I stood on my seat; the water swirled around my neck and ruthlessly kept rising. I was submerged again! I could vaguely see my surroundings but was aware of panicking people nearby.

The amazing thing was, during this entire under water experience, I was extremely calm and peaceful, and I did not even have to hold my breath!

I kept thinking about the words the captain said, 'all will be perfectly fine.'

Finally, the swell was over, the water level went down, and we came out into the freedom of the vast calm ocean; all was back to normal.

I touched my clothes – they were not even wet! I looked around the boat and everything was dry!

We sailed along with ease, the difficulty behind and looking forward to our longed-for destination.

The dream ended.

Immediately these words from Isaiah 43:2 filled my mind, **'When you pass through the waters, I will be with you; and through the rivers, they shall not overwhelm you; when you walk through fire you shall not be burned and the flame shall not consume you.'**

Jonah (despite his disobedience) was protected by the Almighty God who provided a great fish so he wouldn't drown. Instead, in his unusual temporary home, he was brought closer to God and promised to do as he was told!

In Daniel 3 we read the familiar story of Shadrach, Meshach and Abednego being thrown into the fiery furnace – hated by their countrymen, but faith in their Almighty God, they stepped into the furnace. On their exit from the fire… v27 – **'the fire had not had any**

power over the bodies of those men. The hair of their heads was not singed, their cloaks were not harmed, and no smell of fire had come upon them.'

Do not panic, worry, or stress during your swell in life – trust the Captain! He is working out His purposes so that we will live to glorify Him on earth and one day reach our eternal and glorious destination!

8
Lights in the Long Dark Tunnel

I had on many occasions heard children of the King speak of a long dark tunnel they had endured at some stage in their lives. However, never did I imagine our family would be thrown into such.

In no way had I considered until now how horrible that experience would be; scary, lonely, traumatic, wearisome, unknown, black… to name a few!

I also never understood or realised the blessings that would be possible in a long dark tunnel; peace, provision, protection, guidance, counsel, liberation, strength, joy (you read right, yes joy!)... to name a few.

This was only doable by the presence of Jesus and the truth of God's Word becoming a reality and saturating our thoughts daily; on numerous occasions, hourly. In fact, in those early months we spent most of the day (and night) reading, reciting and repeating verse after verse, chapter and chapter, Psalm after Psalm. The Bible and the presence of Jesus was our lifeline, helping us try to make sense of the turmoil we were plunged into. As time went on, any longer than one hour absent from reading or dwelling on scripture became unbearable. Satan would strike with his attacks, and we immediately spoke out scripture until the peace of God filled our home once again.

Praise God for His word! It truly does bring life, gives courage, peace, and calm through the toughest of circumstances.

Whatever simple, insignificant, mundane; enormous, major, or torturous situation you may be going through, I encourage you – before you go to a person – go to your Heavenly Father! His counsel is priceless, genuine, confidential, and reliable.

* * * * *

The following are just some of the scriptures that provided light for us through our long tunnel. Pray over them for your situation right now and be truly blessed as you dwell on and realise the wonderful truth of these for your life right now.

I have tried to order them as best I could as and when the Lord gave them to us – in His perfect timing. I have highlighted parts of each verse that took on a completely new dimension as never before. An entire new reality that has been engraved on our minds forever. Only for the tunnel, I believe we would not have been blessed in this way!

'**Be still** and **know** that **I am God**' (Psalm 45:10).

'So do not fear, for **I am with you**; do not be dismayed, for **I am your God.** I will strengthen you and help you; **I will uphold you** with my righteous right hand' (Isaiah 41:10).

'What then shall we say to these things? If God is for us, **who can be against us**?' (Romans 8:31)

'Finally, **be strong in the Lord** and in the strength of his might. **Put on the whole armour** of God, that you may be **able to stand against** the schemes of the devil. For we do not wrestle against flesh and blood, but against the rulers, against the **spiritual forces** of evil in the heavenly places' (Ephesians 6:10-12).

'But Jesus looked at them and said, "with **man** this is impossible, but with **God** all things are possible"' (Matthew 19:26).

'When I am afraid, **I put my trust in you**.' (Psalm 56:3).

'Do not be afraid, **little flock**, for **your Father** has been pleased to **give you the kingdom**' (Luke 12:32).

'But **He knows** the way that I take; when he has tested me, **I will come forth as gold**' (Job 23:10).

'Though he **slay me**, yet will **I hope in him**…' (Job 13:15).

'I can do **everything** through Christ who gives me strength' (Philippians 4:13).

'Now to Him who is able to do **immeasurably more** than all we ask or imagine, according to **his power that is at work within us**' (Ephesians 3:20).

'I have been crucified with Christ and **I no longer live**, but Christ lives in me' (Galatians 2:20).

'As for you, **you meant evil** against me, but **God meant it for good**' (Genesis 50:20).

'But those **who hope** (wait) in the Lord will renew their strength. They will **soar on wings** like eagles; they will run and **not grow weary**. They will walk and **not be faint**' (Isaiah 41:31).

'Do not be anxious about anything, but in **everything** by prayer and supplication with **thanksgiving** let your requests be made known to God and the peace of God, which **surpasses all understanding,** will **guard your hearts and your minds** in Christ Jesus' (Philippians 4:6).

'**Rejoice** in the Lord **always**; again, I will say **rejoice**' (Philippians 4:4).

'"My grace is **sufficient for you**, for my power is made perfect in weakness." Therefore, I will boast more gladly of my weaknesses, so that the **power of Christ** may rest upon me' (2 Corinthians 12:9).

'You keep him in **perfect peace** whose mind is **stayed** on you, because he **trusts** in you' (Isaiah 26:3-4).

'And we know that for those who love God **all** things work together **for good**, for those who are called according to **his purpose**' (Romans 8:28).

'For **I know the plans** I have for you, declares the Lord, plans for welfare and not for evil, to give you a future and a hope' (Jeremiah 29:11).

God's Word certainly was a lamp to our feet and a light to our path through this long, dark and seemingly, never-ending tunnel.

God blessed us with many other little lights on this journey of darkness; far too many to share and because of the volume – many I have sadly forgotten.

Lots, however, I will never forget! The following is a skeleton account of numerous other little lights along the way:

Handwritten letters and cards were posted through our letter box. We cherished each one, knowing that behind the words was a person or couple who cared, who loved, who prayed – these blessed us, beyond words.

E-mails, WhatsApp, text, and messenger messages – each one we read with much appreciation and joy in our hearts. We will always be grateful for these brothers and sisters in Christ who stood with us on this unknown journey.

The beautiful thing was that none of the senders knew anything of the stress we were going through. As was advised, we hadn't shared any of the situation that we were enduring. However, these friends who were genuine disciples of Jesus didn't need to know; they just loved us and prayed, as commanded in God's Word. This was a huge challenge and blessing to us.

We are truly grateful for those who met with us and prayed with us, such individuals displayed a wise and godly character. We enjoyed friendship and fellowship on these occasions and as we thanked them for their prayers; they said what we needed: 'We are and will continue to pray for you at this time of stress and difficulty.' Praise God for these individuals who, unknown to them, were lights in our very dark tunnel.

Church was difficult throughout these years; we knew where we wanted to be, but God worked it that we could not be there. At the end of each week, we would pray and ask our Sovereign Father where He would have us to worship. It was always the right place! Our hearts were encouraged, blessed, and challenged and we grew spiritually from the teaching, worship, and refreshment of fellowship. Praise God for many sermons that were a perfect fit for what we needed to hear on that Sunday morning. More little lights sent from our loving Heavenly Father to brighten the tunnel!

On a few Sunday morning worship services, however, we encountered a severe deadness and lack of God's Holy Spirit to be present. It wasn't church at all; just an organised operation, as we saw it. These experiences were good, teaching us much and enlightening us about our own spiritual needs and blessings.

9
The Blessing of A B C

In the waiting, many miles were covered by car, miles that were not wasted, but used to bless us and keep us aware of the presence of Jesus.

We listened to podcasts (mainly John Piper and Alastair Begg), we fell in love with the biblical truths and uplifting worship of Sovereign Grace music and spent many miles listening to God's Word online and praying (with our eyes open!).

Perhaps one of the greatest blessings of all was playing the A B C game! It was pure, spirit-filled Scripture and each time it was played the presence of Jesus was very close – tangibly close.

The game was for us to take turns to work through, from A to Z – shouting out, 'Who we are in Christ,' or 'What Christ has done for us.'

It's a super game to play to pass the time when travelling and reinforces the depth of the attributes of God and the blessing of who we are in Him.

I would like to share an example with you:

A – Adopted

'He predestined us for adoption to Himself as sons through Jesus Christ, according to the purpose of His will.' (Ephesians 1:5)

B – Blessed

'Blessed is the man who trusts in the Lord, whose trust is the Lord.' (Jeremiah 17:7)

C – Chosen

'You did not choose me, but I chose you and appointed you so that you might go and bear fruit – fruit that will last and so that whatever you ask in my name the Father will give you.' (John 15:16)

D – Delivered

'He has delivered us from the domain of darkness and transferred us to the kingdom of His beloved Son.' (Colossians 1:13)

E – Empowered

'For God has not given us a spirit of fear, but of power and of love and of a sound mind.' (2 Timothy 1:7)

F – Forgiven

'In Him we have redemption through his blood, the forgiveness of sins, in accordance with the riches of God's grace' (Ephesians 1:7).

G – Grace Given

'But He said to me, "My grace is sufficient for you, for my power is made perfect in weakness"' (2 Corinthians

12:9).

H – Hidden

'Set your minds on things that are above, not on things that are on earth. For you have died and your life is hidden with Christ in God' (Colossians 3:2-3).

I – Instructed

'I will instruct you and teach you in the way that you should go; I will counsel you with my eye upon you' (Psalm 32:8).

J – Justified

'Therefore, since we have been justified by faith, we have peace with God through our Lord Jesus Christ' (Romans 5:1).

K – Kept

'… to those who are called, beloved in God the Father and kept for Jesus Christ' (Jude 1:1).

L – Loved

'But God shows His love for us in that while we were still sinners, Christ died for us' (Romans 5:8).

M – Mighty

'I can do all things through Him who strengthens me' (Philippians 4:13).

N – New creation

'Therefore, if anyone is in Christ, he is a new creation' (2 Corinthians 5:17).

O – One with Christ

'For you are all one in Christ Jesus' (Galatians 3:28).

P – Protected

'He will not let your foot slip – He who watches over you will not slumber' (Psalm 121:3).

Q – Qualified

'Giving thanks to the Father, who has qualified you to share in the inheritance of the saints in light' (Colossians 1:12).

R – Redeemed

'Christ redeemed us from the curse of the law by becoming a curse for us' (Galatians 3:13).

S – Satisfied

'Bless the Lord, O my soul and all that is within me, bless His holy name! Bless the Lord, O my soul and forget not all his benefits, who forgives all your iniquity, who heals all your diseases, who redeems your life from the pit, who crowns you with steadfast love and mercy, who satisfies you with good so that your youth is renewed like the eagle's' (Psalm 103:1-5).

T – Treasured

'For you are a people holy to the Lord your God and the Lord has chosen you to be a people for his treasured possession' (Deuteronomy 14:2).

U – Unique

'For you formed my inward parts, you knitted me

together in my mother's womb' (Psalm 139:13).

V – Victorious

'But thanks be to God, who gives us the victory through our Lord Jesus Christ' (1 Corinthians 15:57).

W – Wonderfully Made

'I praise you, for I am fearfully and wonderfully made' (Psalm 139:14).

X – Crucified in Christ

'I have been crucified with Christ. It is no longer I who live, but Christ who lives in me' (Galatians 2:20).

Y – Yoked with Christ

'Take my yoke upon you and learn from me, for I am gentle and lowly in heart and you will find rest for your souls' (Matthew 11:29).

Z – Zealous

'Who gave himself for us to redeem us from all lawlessness and to purify for himself a people for his own possession who are zealous for good works' (Titus 2:14).

Why not try this game on your next journey? You and those travelling with you will be enriched in the presence of your Saviour.

10
Perfect Timing

September 2020

It hit me like a strong northernly (taking one off their feet) wind! Matthew had wanted to and had suggested several times he may resign but this time he knew it was what he *must* do!

We prayed and wept together as we contemplated the end of a chapter. The resignation e-mail was written with a heavy heart, yet immediate peace filled our hearts and again, that still small voice was reassuring that we were walking in His will – in *His* timing – not in 2017 as we would have liked; not in 2018 as we would have liked; not in 2019…

In the days that followed, one may expect with having made such a huge decision, to feel vulnerable, worried, stressed, anxious… but no – God's word reminded us that **'He knows the way that I take….' Job 23:10.** All we needed to do was to trust and 'enjoy the journey that He would set before us'.

I'm not going to lie; these were tough days! Very tough days. But very tough days with Jesus are restful days; grazing on the luscious green food of His words that consumed into the deepest depths of our beings. Praise Him!

I wasn't really surprised that yet again I took things into my own hands. We were losing our home that came with Matthew's job, so to gain some control in the situation, I started to search for a place to rent near our two daughters and their families… God had other plans; a much better plan!

You see, our lives are a constant and daily throwing of self into the safe hands of our Shepherd. Trusting that He knows what He is doing and has it already planned – a beautiful plan! For us, a plan we would never have imagined, but a plan that was timely, complete, and perfect for this season.

Over that summer my father (91) wasn't in his usual top form; we were concerned. My sister suggested that perhaps the previous cancer had returned and to his oesophagus this time.

Just a few days after the resignation letter was e-mailed my father rang and asked me if we would consider going to live with him. I was speechless! Then came the logically thought-out phrase, 'No, definitely not Daddy, there wouldn't be room!' He proceeded to suggest there was plenty of room; we would have the upstairs and sitting room. He had it all sorted in true 'Daddy' style. When Matthew found out about Dad's (God's) plan, he said, 'Why not?' Matthew reminded me how Daddy was in touch with his Saviour and had most definitely been praying for the Lord to guide us. I had to agree – there were no truer words!

This was another huge decision; lots of prayer and a solid confirmation would be needed.

Together, with our family and our Sovereign Father we made our decision.

Two weeks later Daddy spoke to me again. 'Did you think any more of coming to stay with me?'

'Yes, we did,' I replied quickly. 'If it's okay, we will come and stay with you.' Again, in typical 'Daddy' style, he was overcome with emotion. God had answered his prayer.

As I continued to work (now that's another provision story!), Matthew packed and moved all our earthly processions (with our children and friend's help), to Hazeldene – my childhood home.

God's peace is certainly not limited to one place! His peace and His presence moved with us, overwhelming at times, in this unexpected step.

In the evenings of the following year that was to follow, Daddy shared with us his antics as a child and many interesting facts about the area and home place we both now called 'home'. These were special times, planned by our Heavenly Father who even cares about the simplest, unimportant, yet meaningful details in life.

'Perfect Timing' I have called this chapter – we didn't fully comprehend this at the time, but as the weeks unfolded it was very much realised.

Perfect, in that within a few days of moving I was offered a job as a one-to-one teaching assistant in a local primary school for the rest of the school year.

As the following summer ended, I had nothing sorted for the new school year. I sat back and rested in the strong hands of my Sovereign Heavenly Father. In August I received a call from the same principal asking if I had got sorted for the new school year. To make a long, yet beautiful story short, God had yet again blessed me with a job (which months later became permanent!), with a fabulous little 7-year-old. God willing it would be my privilege to support, help, teach and care for this child until they finished primary school. I prayed this child would see Jesus daily and come to love Him personally.

How good is God!

Also, perfect timing, in that Dad's health deteriorated, and he needed someone to live with him.

How good is God!

You may not understand what God is presently allowing to happen to you, your family, your spouse… but you can trust Him. It is biblically okay to ask, how? Why? What? When? Job and David did – so can we!

Our Sovereign Father, on the other hand, *does* understand, He *does* know how, why, what and when! His ways are always perfect, beautiful and in precise timing.

Trust Him!

11
An Unexpected Privilege

Over the years God has given me many privileges; privileges that I won't name, but privileges that I *must* thank God for allowing me to have. For health, resources, courage, strength, wisdom, guidance, grace… to carry out every privilege, I give God praise.

I will, however, mention the privilege of being a daughter of the King. A daughter of godly parents: Robert and Mary Wilson. Wife to Matthew, who I greatly admire for his solid trust in His precious Saviour. Mum to three godly children and mum-in-law to their spouses. Granny to four handsome grandsons and three beautiful granddaughters. Friend to some of the best disciples of Jesus – I am blessed beyond words!

One privilege; very unexpected but one of the most blessed! Caring for Daddy in his 92nd and final year on earth.

Just weeks after Matthew and I had moved in with Dad, he got an appointment letter to go into hospital for an endoscopy test in his oesophagus.

January 2021

As he and I travelled, a quiet calm atmosphere was present. We talked about the nature in the fields around us, and oh yes, the crazy young drivers speeding past.

The procedure was all done and dusted in a relatively short time and soon we were alone, in a large, empty and darkened ward, waiting on the consultant to give the results. Calmness continued to prevail, and Dad reminded me that it was all in better hands.

The consultant confirmed our fears – yes, it was cancer – a large tumour had been found. After a short question and answer session and a further rest for Dad, we headed home, this time in silence – pondering – yet still with the calm assurance that Jesus was with us and Dad's health was safely in the control of our Sovereign Father.

'Do not be anxious about anything, but in everything by prayer and supplication with thanksgiving let your requests be made known to God. And the peace of God, which surpasses all understanding, will guard your hearts and your minds in Christ Jesus.' – Philippians 4:6-7

This scripture rattled through my head in the hours and days that were to follow; desperately grasping not to be anxious but rather to trust as another blow shocked me on the journey!

With the strength of God's Holy Spirit, trust is what I did.

I had been learning the value of changing my anxiety

to trust. Oh, what beauty is in that word, what liberation! Bringing peace, comfort, acceptance and even joy.

I cannot think of a more suitable verse in Scripture to memorise and repeat than Philippians 4:6-7. It turns painful, uncontrollable, life-changing news into a calm, restful and God-controlled reality.

What is your shock on your journey? Disappointment? Loss? Betrayal? Persecution? Illness? Hardship?

Philippians 4: 6-7 is Scripture that will:

- Refocus your mind.
- Take you through.
- Give you inner peace.
- Guard you.
- Overflow your life with joy.

Do not be anxious. Obey this command and your worst situation will be turned into a blessing!

Over the following weeks, numerous phone calls needed to be made, questions asked, assessments carried out and carers put in place. Furniture changed around, diet readjusted, and weakness grew.

Eight months later, on November 9th at his home of 81 years, Daddy went to see his Precious Saviour. Two days later, with heavy yet peaceful hearts we said a temporary goodbye. Until we meet again!

The funeral service was triumphant and focused on the Saviour who had just welcomed another sinner into His perfect home – saved by grace and now made perfect in totality.

Caring for Dad – a privilege I would never have had if the journey of pain, trauma and loss had not have happened to us.

12
Give, Take Away, but Give Back Even More!

The weeks, months and indeed year which was to follow transpired in grief not only for the passing of a parent but also, agonising grief over the very unexpected conclusion to our long, dark tunnel.

This wasn't how it was to finish, well, so we were led to believe! How come? Why? What's going to happen to us now? The questions were many but again that special still small voice was heard, yet again, over and above the loud and deafening lies of the enemy. No, our precious Saviour did not give us answers but He did give us calm as we clung onto His word: **'For my thoughts are not your thoughts, neither are your ways my ways, declares the Lord. For as the heavens are higher than the earth, so are my ways higher than your ways and my thoughts than your thoughts.' – Isaiah 55:8-9**

God's way had turned out to be exactly the opposite of what our way would have been. We had to keep trusting, more than ever, our Sovereign Heavenly

Father. We had done exactly so up to this point, we would trust now, and by the help of our precious Jesus we would continue to trust, no matter what!

* * * * *

As a married couple God had given us so much, over many years; lots more than we ever needed, deserved, expected, and truly appreciated. But now, God had taken much of that away; our loss – humongous! The list– endless! Loss of our home, church family, a few friends, other relationships, ministry, reputation, financial security, lifestyle…

At a time like this it's comforting and liberating to keep in mind the words of an old, yet powerful song – 'The steadfast love of the Lord never ceases, His mercies never come to an end, they are new every morning, new every morning, great is your faithfulness.'

That is exactly the amazing love our Heavenly Father demonstrated to us. It is very difficult for me to put into words just how good, loving and gracious God has been to us through this dark, unknown, horrendous, yet planned, long tunnel. However, I am aware that even though we lost much, we gained much more! What a truly faithful, compassionate, and gracious Father.

Some of the blessings since our world was turned upside down in 2017:

- A deeper relationship with Jesus.
- A greater awareness of the daily presence of the Father, Son, and Holy Spirit.

- A stronger and more beautiful relationship with my husband.
- A life changing realization of how PRAYER and PRAISE can bring me triumphantly through any situation that I will ever encounter.
- The delight of three very adorable little granddaughters and a very cute little baby grandson, to add to our oldest three fabulous grandsons.
- Our son and family moving back to Northern Ireland from England in 2022. It is so good to have them close by.
- The joy of having a closer bond with our children and their families.
- Being able to buy my homeplace (Hazeldene) and having the thrill of putting our own mark on it.
- A new church family.
- New friends.
- New jobs.
- New privileges and opportunities.
- New opportunities to serve.
- Financial stability.

If you love the Lord, no matter what your circumstances, God will remain faithful; loving us more than we will ever understand or deserve! More than we could ever show to those around us – even our nearest and dearest.

He hears our cry for help, forgiveness, blessing, instruction, peace and gives unconditionally with abundant provisions piled on! Praise Him!

Conclusion

'I will choose to enjoy the journey that God has set before me.' The challenge of this message on the card sent to us in September 2014 penetrated my heart frequently throughout this trial. With God's help I chose to enjoy a painful experience for the glory of God. Yes, it is possible to know joy, even in a season of suffering! – but only with Jesus by our side.

* * * * *

I was aware that God wanted me to honour and give Him glory through writing this little book. Somehow, in a way to combat the potential opposite that appeared to be happening. I sat and scribbled down the possibility of 24 chapters. I started to write. However, getting to chapter 10, I felt I should soon conclude and so I entrust to God the change of the original plan of a longer book.

Life's a bit like that, isn't it? What we think our life might look like, as it progresses is often changed by the perfect intervention of the Almighty Creator! The only one who knows all things and the only one who knows what is best to make us more like Jesus.

* * * * *

Matthew and I have had the privilege of serving our Saviour in a full-time capacity for over 32 years! What a joy, to see children, young people and adults come to know Jesus and grow in Him through various means of outreach and ministry.

On our ministry journey, we have made many mistakes and on occasions have been guilty of pride, and serving in our own strength. However, despite our failings and sin, we know that God in His great mercy and grace accomplished much for His glory in these years. For this we praise Him and trust to His keeping these precious persons for the honour and glory of His name.

In the latter six years we have not been in full-time Christian ministry in the way we were before, however we have been blessed with a much greater honour – 'time' and therefore the joy of getting to know, in a much deeper and precious way, the Jesus we served for these years. It's rather ironic really, but true! After all, that is what our tough and unexpected long tunnel was all about. The answer to my prayer back in the spring of 2017, that we would both know God better and be radiant for Him. This has happened, at least the first! My prayer is that we will be more and more radiant for our Saviour each day, walking in His way, until that great day when we will stand before Him – completely perfect and about to commence a forever eternity with Him.

"Surely, I am coming soon." Amen. Come Lord Jesus!'

The journey continues...

Thank You

To Matthew, my husband and earthly best friend; for proofreading these pages and guiding in the detail of the story and scripture.

To our adult children who have graciously, lovingly, and non-judgementally walked this journey with us. Always praying, supporting, and showing Jesus.

To a gentleman, from day one, who was a constant, non-judgemental, engaging, pastoral support. We loved to see you come for a chat and cuppa; always sitting in the same spot in the living room! You know who you are; we will always thank God for your gracious, genuine, and unconditional compassionate care.

Finally, and most importantly:

To the only wise God our Saviour, be glory and majesty, dominion and power, both now and ever. Amen.

Contact

As we journey through life we all face different trials.

Times when God uses adversity to draw us closer to Him, mould us to be more like Jesus and fulfil His purposes for us.

Often these trials may feel overwhelming.

If you are finding it difficult to enjoy your present journey and need someone to confidentially pray for you, please contact me at

choosetoenjoy@gmail.com

Milton Keynes UK
Ingram Content Group UK Ltd.
UKHW030105141223
434291UK00016B/1044